Text by Kristi V. Johnson
Illustrations by Ananta Mohanta

ISBN: 979-8-218-46324-3

Designed and formatted by Ryan Webb.

First edition 2024.

ABC
Dance and Move
with Me

Written by
Kristi V. Johnson

Illustrated by
Ananta Mohanta

In **a**cro dance I can tumble and twirl.

I will be a great **b**allerina and dance all over the world.

Beads, bows, and ruffles on each Costume I see.

My sister and I learned a **duet** to a nursery rhyme medley.

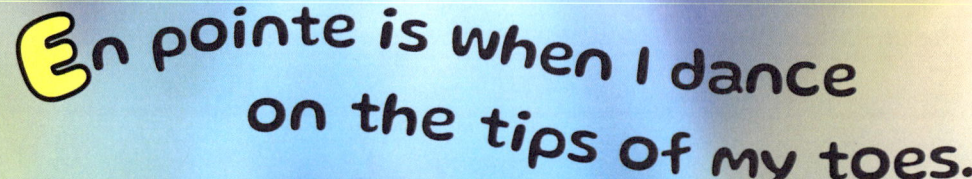

En pointe is when I dance
on the tips of my toes.

Freestyle dancing lets me move freely to the music and strike any pose.

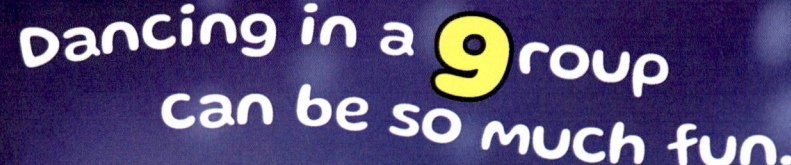

Dancing in a **g**roup
can be so much fun.

Cheer me on in this **h**ip hop battle, one-on-one.

A dancer uses their imagination to explore new moves.

Jazz dance is all about the rhythm and finding the groove.

In a **K**ickline, the legs are straight with the toes to the sky.

I **L**eap with my arms stretched out, because I believe I can fly.

The **M**usic is in rhythm with the beat of my heart.

When I hear the umbers 5, 6, 7, 8,
I know it's time to start.

Onstage is where
the dance comes alive.

We use **P**rops like scarves, hats, or cool glasses to cover our eyes.

The **Q**uickstep runs,
skips, hops, and flicks.

In dance class, a reverence is a curtsy or bow done before we are dismissed.

Dancers use their body parts to make **Shapes**, like circles, triangles, and squares.

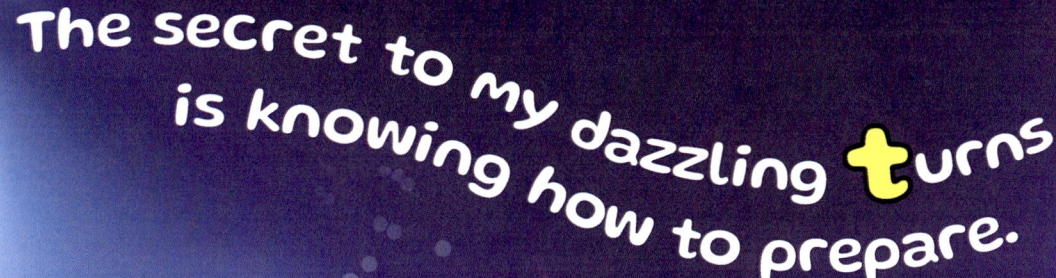

The secret to my dazzling turns is knowing how to prepare.

We are moving in **U**nison,
in sync from head to toe.

My first ballet **V**ariation is from a story that happened a long time ago.

Before class, my teacher helps me Warm up my feet at the barre.

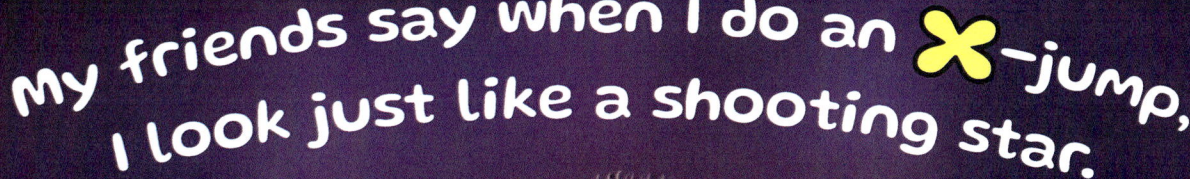

My friends say when I do an **X**-jump,
I look just like a shooting star.

I pretend my **y**oga mat is a garden, as I sit in butterfly pose and flap my wings.

In **Z**umba, the rhythm is the teacher
as we laugh, dance, play, and sing.

A – Acro Dance

B – Ballerina

C – Costumes

D – Duet

E – En Pointe

F – Freestyle

G – Group

H – Hip Hop

I – Imagination

J – Jazz Dance

K – Kickline

L – Leap

M – Music

N – Numbers

O – Onstage

P – Props

Q – Quickstep

R – Reverence

S – Shapes

T – Turns

U – Unison

V – Variation

W – Warm-up

X – X-Jump

Y – Yoga

Z – Zumba